POETIC SCRIPTURES

(THE LIFE, GROWTH AND JOURNEY)

MICHAEL E. WILLIAMS

P.O.M. Publishing Co.
Dolton, Illinois

Table of Contents

Acknowledgements
Introduction

PART ONE: LIFE AND REALITY

PART TWO: LOVE AND PAIN

PART THREE: GROWTH AND INSPIRATION

Biography
Contact Information

"Fear is weakness, learn from what experience teaches." - Nas

Acknowledgements

I would first like to thank God for his mercy and grace. Thank you Father for covering me with your blood. I realize that without you I am nothing. Thank you also for all favor and blessings in my life.

I am grateful to have been raised by both parents. My mother Luvenia Williams, thank you for all the love and support. To my father Dr. Norton C. Williams you have instilled in me discipline, wisdom and knowledge throughout my life. Love you both!

To my caring son Elijah, you are a big part of my success and the reason that I will continue to work hard. Thank you for always encouraging me and telling me to work on my poetry. Love you son!

Special thanks to my Pastor LaToyia Elston. God has really used you to uplift and change my life forever. Love you Pastor and need you to survive!

To the greatest motivator on earth Lamont Brown Sr. Thanks for mentoring me and taking me under your wings. You have always been one of my greatest inspirations during my journey. Love you Bro!

Special thanks to my P.O.E.T family and mentor Blaq Ice. I really do look up to you and appreciate all the knowledge that you have passed down. Thanks for pushing me to always work harder. And to all the talented poets and artists that I have shared the stage with, it's been a pleasure. Peace and love to you all!

A special thanks to the following that have been uplifting throughout my journey; Elder Robert Marshall, Jazzy Jazz, Mary Javier, Derious Smith, Michelle Bowen, Vincent Silmon Jr., Anicya Henderson, Rodney Trussell, Mischa Terry, Street Prophet, Steven Mosley, Carol Davis Mottley, Tony Herron and the entire Saved by Grace family. Love you all and need you to survive!

Special thanks to authors Fabulous Fe and Poetess Kottyn. Also LaTasha Jackson for assisting me with publishing my book. Without you all it would have not been possible to get everything done this year!

Thank you to all of my siblings, family and friends near and far.

Last but not least, a special thanks to the person that told me I would never write a book. Thank you for the motivation!

"I can't die without striving to fulfill my purpose. If I do, I would have lived a life that was worthless."
– Terishanda Brown

Introduction

Poetic Scriptures was inspired from the sudden loss of my younger sister Larenya who passed away, March 19th of 1999. This book poetically shows you my most difficult times, how I persevered and overcame through faith and poetry. Poetic Scriptures enlightens you on how I came about writing each chapter in my life and what inspired me to write at that present time. Poetic Scriptures also gives you a biblical scripture that can somehow relate to each experience. I express my thoughts and emotions about testimonies throughout my life; from reality, love, pain, growth and inspiration. When it's all said and done this book will make you think, sometimes laugh, cry, be inspired and be uplifted as you can relate to different experiences in your life as well.

"We have to position ourselves for the promises of God."   -Pastor LaToyia Elston

Part One: Life and Reality

Life and Death

As I walk through the valley of the shadow of death, at times I feel fearful don't know when I'm going to take my last breath, don't be afraid it's easy to say, watching the channel five news a little girl got rapped today, some cold-hearted youngsters just did a drive-by with no conscience not caring who gets hit and die, loved ones left with guilt and tears asking why, in the wrong place at the wrong time, now it's hard to face reality wishing everything could rewind, "shorty was ten and innocent tell me why they have to kill,"? another funeral I just guess it was all in God's will, our brothers and sisters working hard striving to make it, money coming in only for someone evil and jealous to stick them up and take it, selling drugs to our children and telling them that the gang is where they belong, then there's no father to show them how to keep a straight head, "shorty don't let nobody steer you wrong," another mother left to raise her kids alone, our daughters growing up too fast choosing what time they should come home, "asking myself when all this hatred gone end,"? then it's hard to trust the next man I thought he was my friend, believing in a higher power but yet thoughts of caring a gun, spirit speaking to me saying "Michael you know that's not in the will of God son" so I'm left praying for angels to watch over me another day, this world is corrupt we need true teachers and preachers to show us the wise-way, we have to elevate and renew our minds and begin to think more positive, I just made it out my twenties but I haven't even began to live, though this walk is not easy, I'm just being real and honest, hoping to fulfill at-least the seventy-years I was promised, though at times my heart is heavy, another trial, another test, my baby-sister took all she could bare so now in peace she rest, though I'm trying not to cry, I got to be strong, steadily keeping my head up cause life goes on, "God is my refuge and strength," I heard those words in a sermon, I've made a lot of mistakes but I'm still understanding and learning, I have to watch where I go, be quick to listen and slow to speak, at times I get provoked but I must remain humble and meek, cause I've been told to be wise as a serpent and harmless as a dove, there's always going to be enemies and haters but you still show them love, Satan trying to hinder me I hear him talking, but he can't get to me I'm still righteously walking, cause I've been given the spirit of power, love and a sound mind, so I'm gone keep on stepping until it's my time.

my testimony

I was inspired to write this poem one evening after watching all the violence and chaos on channel five news. It was heartbreaking watching the gang wars, little girls being rapped, children coming up missing as well as the political and constant religious wars amongst our people. I was truly saddened as I wrote with a lot of anger and pain. I can't begin to understand how we can hate so much to rob, steal and kill one-another. As the poem ended I became uplifted realizing that I'm blessed to still be alive and to have my right mind.

Proverbs 3:1-2

My son, forget not my law; but let thine heart keep my commandments: 2 for length of days, and long life, and peace shall they add to thee.

A Letter to Baby-Sister

It's not easy writing this all down on paper, I had to second guess, I just can't keep it all inside I have to get it off my chest, hard to say it out loud, I know you can't hear it, even though at times I do feel you in spirit, some things I should of did, some words I should of said but I never said it, looking back now, I truly regret it, I wish I would of known your condition or seen a sign, diabetes taking you out at twenty-years old it never crossed my mind, so suddenly so fast, the doctors say it was of sudden-cause, trying to figure it all out I had to sit down and pause, rolling you out on a stretcher it was hard seeing you go, covered in white as I watched from the living room window, that was one day I didn't want to believe, you had dreams and goals you never got to achieve, looking down over your casket I took one last look at your face, I knew it wasn't possible but for you to live on I would of sacrificed and took your place, comparing my life to yours I didn't understand, but God has his purpose I know it's all in his hands

But this is A Letter to you Baby-Sister, I want you to know that I love you and I really miss you, still thinking about you in the bed as I lay, I had to write you this letter even though I know you long gone away

Though at the time it didn't seem that fair, I know you had plans to go to Cosmetology School and keep styling hair, losing you so young is what made it so sad, even though I reminisce about the good memories we had, growing up in our childhood we use to play ball off the wall, we would always laugh every time someone would trip and fall, we use to ride our bikes and play tag in the park, hide and go seek and catch lightning bugs after dark, I remember running-bases and four-squares, playing Pac-Man on the Atari and musical chairs, red light green light, we use to watch "Sesame Street" and "Bozo," "In Living Color" and on Saturday nights we'd always stay up late to watch the "Apollo," in '91' we cheered as the (Bulls) beat the (Lakers), you use to always walk to the store for me to get my newspapers, watching the airplanes take off and driving down to the lake, it use to smell good from the kitchen it was the cookies you baked, you not being around it seems kind of strange, wishing you were still here so you can see how things have changed, it's your laughter and pretty smile that I will always miss, you affected my life in such an emotional way, but I guess it had to come to this, I know we had some altercations but I never meant no harm, you will always be in my heart and forever will Baby-Sister be tattooed on my arm.

my testimony

"A Letter to Baby-Sister" was the first poem that I ever wrote at the age of 21. It was inspired from the sudden and tragic loss of my younger sister (Larenya) who passed away March 19th of 1999. Just months after her funeral I wanted to express my grief, so I began to write her a letter and it turned into poetry. That was a night that I will never forget.

RIP Baby-Sister

Psalms 103:2-5

Bless the Lord, O my soul, and forget not all his benefits: who forgiveth all thine iniquities; who healeth all diseases; Who redeemeth thy life from destruction: who crowneth thee with loving-kindness and tender mercies; Who satisfies your mouth with good things; so that thy youth is renewed like the eagle's.

<u>MY POETRY</u>

*THIS IS MY POETRY, MY POETRY, MY SIGHTS, MY DREAMING
NIGHTS, MY DEEPEST THOUGHTS, MY UNRIGHTEOUS FAULTS,
FROM CARNAL TO SPIRITUALITY, FROM PURITY TO SEXUALITY,
ITS LIFE AND DEATH, THE PEOPLE THAT PAST ON, THE ONE'S
THAT'S LEFT, WISDOM AND KNOWLEDGE, THE CHURCHES, THE
ELDERS, THE COLLEGE, THE MUSIC, THE LYRICS, THE BEATS, THE
GANGSTERS, THE DEALERS, THE STREETS, RELIGION AND
POLITICS, THE INMATES, THE DICS, LOVE AND HATE, YOUR
MIND STATE, RIGHT AND WRONG, PEOPLE'S LIVES CUT SHORT,
SOME LIVED LONG, HEAVEN AND HELL, FREEDOM OR JUST
LOCKED IN A CELL, DARKNESS, LIGHT, TURN THE OTHER CHEEK,
NAW FIGHT; FAITH, DOUBT, IN SIN, WITHOUT, IT'S THE
BEGINNING, THE END, YOUR ENEMY, YOUR FRIEND, BEING
POOR, TO MONEY AND FAME, THE SUNSHINE, THE RAIN, MIND-
ELEVATION OR JUST STAYING THE SAME, JEW OR GENTILE, IN
BELIEF OR IN DENIAL, GOD OR MAN, YOUR TRUST WHICH
HAND, FALL, STAND, I WANT TO, I CAN, PEACE, DESTRUCTION IN
THE MIDDLE EAST, HAM, SHAM, IT'S THE I AM THAT I AM, THE
LAND, THE NATIONS, THE BOOK OF DANIEL AND REVELATIONS,
THE PROPHECY, THE THEOLOGY, YOU, ME, BLIND OR SEE,
IGNORE, TAKE HEED, PICK UP A BOOK, LEARN, READ, FAIL OR
SUCCEED? THE ARROGANT, THE HUMBLE ON ONE KNEE, THE
REAL, THE PHONY, THE IN LOVE, THE LONELY, THE LOVE FOR
GOD, THE LOVE FOR A SHE, AS MY BROTHER THE LOVE FOR A
HE, MY LIFE AND WHAT I'M DESTINED TO BE, MY WORDS, MY
LYRICS, THIS IS MY POETRY.*

my testimony

"My Poetry" was inspired by the love and passion that I have for writing. I'm basically expressing all the different poems that I write giving choices that determine our future. I also show how we can be in a different state of mind during the course of our lives. I came about writing a lot of poems from having dreams, visions and just being in deep thought.

1 Kings 4:32

And He spake three thousand proverbs: and his songs were a thousand and five.

Righteous Path

Walking this Righteous Path, you have to find the right road, keep changing your ways, keep searching your soul, so much confusion walking this path; God show me which way to go

My enemies want to harm me, no fear I'm now in God's army, they coming from all angles, five on two I'm protected by my guardian angels, I have dominion, what you think of me, I don't need your opinion, judgmental minds but we all sinning at times, some great, some small we need to help each-other cause the creator's gone judge us all, even though hatred is hard to measure, I can't see how one can kill for pleasure, you have to care for yourself first, living by the sword, soon you'll be leaving in a hearse, you need a sound mind or it gets worse, your soul the devil trying to steal, the Bible prophecies you better believe it's all real, prosperity and success, I don't want to see nobody fail, peace and joy, I don't want to see nobody go to hell, even though it seems like we already in it, all of this corruption the devil sent it, the pit is a horrible place, soon looking to see Jesus face to face, from laws to grace, one God one race, from B.C to A.D. it's mathematically when learning theology, things are becoming clearer I'm now beginning to see

Walking this Righteous Path you have to find the right road, keep changing your ways, keep searching your soul, so much confusion walking this path; God show me which way to go

POETIC SCRIPTURES (THE LIFE, GROWTH AND JOURNEY)

People don't stay where they are in life, it's only a phase, taking the right road is a maze, stay willing, one step at a time things start revealing, knowing what's fake, what advice to take, holding on to faith, looking to understand, not knocking my brother but giving him a hand, listening before you speak, realizing the next man hasn't reached his peak, where he is at you was once before, not knowing what God has in store, seek knowledge and you will get more, become wise to different situations, knowing when to stay out of what conversations, putting in place the scriptures correct interpretations, knowing what is sin and what can lead to sin,? saying things right where it doesn't offend, with different people being able to blend, even though you might not know him, encourage him, pray for him, provoke him not to wrath, the Lord is my rod and my staff; only in him I can trust, walking this Righteous Path.

my testimony

"Righteous Path" was inspired from being in different religious conversations while working in the Barbershop. It really helped me by just listening to everyone's opinions and personal beliefs. I was able to share some of my personal feelings about being righteous, as well as the way I see things from my life's teachings.

Romans 1:18

For the wrath of God is revealed from heaven against all ungodliness and unrighteousness of men, who hold the truth in unrighteousness.

<u>Lord I Pray</u>

Lord I Pray not just for myself but for the soldiers in the war zones for the Katrina victims who lost everything including their homes I pray for my son that he works more harder grows up to be a better man than me and my father I pray for the church not the one with the steeple but the righteous one's I'm talking about God's people now humble me Lord as I begin to pray for the evil I pray for every family that's being divided I pray for every soul that's searching but hasn't yet decided I pray for the hopeless to be hopeful to be above average I pray for the drug addicts I pray for every drunkard in the tavern Lord I Pray I pray for the bishops and the leaders not to reach so much for the money but to reach the non-believers I pray more for the priest and for you to touch every School Teacher I pray for the government and their unjust rules even though they took away the Ten-Commandments and prayer out the schools but watch over every child Lord give them direction to choose I even pray for the unborn child the ones that's still in the womb I pray for every street corner every race and every foreigner every denomination or religion give them guidance to break away from tradition I pray for every Bible reader to get a revelation and not just a contradiction I pray for anyone that may be suicidal please Lord give them a reason to keep on living I pray for every thug and drug dealer every prostitute touch her Lord I know only you can heal her I pray for every rapist and every killer to somehow change their ways Lord they need to be delivered I pray for the Hip-Hop Nation give them all a more positive song for the younger Generation I pray for every artist that's trying to make it yea they still waiting but have them to be a little more patient I pray for the job-less I pray for the poor bless them like you bless me Lord as a matter of fact I pray that you bless them more because when we doing well their the one's that we often ignore I pray for the hospitalized and the inmates in prison I pray for every mind even the ones in mental-condition Lord I Pray for the Chicago Police Department every detective and every sergeant I pray for justice in every courtroom every missing child that they come home soon I pray for DCFS every broken hearted mother give them peace and rest strengthen her Lord have her to hold on through every test Lord I Pray that you keep me safe on these dangerous highways I know I've done a lot of wrong Lord but please prolong my days, to Allah, Jehovah, I just pray for your proper name, even though as a child I was taught to do it in Jesus name, just give me understanding because at times it can all seem so strange I just pray you forgive me and for my heart to change, just prepare me Lord to one day see you face to face I do trust you but yet still increase my faith I pray not just for myself but for every poet that ever picks up a mic, guide their tongues Lord give them wisdom and insight, to never give up on poetry just give us more words to write and you know they did us wrong Lord but help us to not hate the whites and on our own kind to stereotype teach us that it's not about that we should be all your children striving to do what's right.

my testimony

"Lord I Pray" was inspired from me not always praying; I really wanted to make up for the lost times that I would go to bed without praying and not acknowledging the Lord.

1 THESSALONIANS 2:2-4

Continue in prayer, and watch in the same with thanksgiving; Withal praying also for us, that God would open unto us a door of utterance, to speak the mystery of Christ, for which I am also in bonds: That I may make it manifest, as I ought to speak.

Troubled Adolescent

An emotional, disturbed, troubled adolescent
Away from juvenile home I was just seconds
Running with the Vice-Lords I wanted to be accepted
Attempts to join but I was already protected
I ran with cliques
Making up gangs the VIP'S and the Palace Pimps
But I was a born leader
What they wouldn't do, I would do it
Right or wrong I just had to prove it
Let's start a lynching
My education was turning to Saturday Schools and
detention
Theft and vandalism
That led to my suspensions
Catching court cases, that's when I had my first vision
I pictured me in prison
A boy amongst unconscious men I had to fix it
I was blessed I dodged strays
Picked up the Barbers Trade
It was at a young teen's age
I was saved, escaped the fast and short life
With the comb, shears, and blades.

my testimony

"Troubled Adolescent" was inspired from just thinking about my childhood and the way that I thought at the time. I was young and always looking to do the wrong things for attention. After being arrested several times I began to wake up and take life in a positive direction by focusing on my trade as a Barber.

Proverbs 22:15

Foolishness is bound up in the heart of a child; but the rod of correction shall drive it far from him.

I Am Reality

I Am Reality, reality of those mentally institutionalized with hallucinations in the mind, injected with medications to keep me from seeing the signs, or is it all illusions as I find solutions to this life-time, to predict what lies ahead and pick what to leave behind, I Am Reality; reality of Christians that's not afraid to speak they mind, you see I question God of answers I have yet to find, he told me to keep living and they will be reveled with time, I Am Reality; reality of those demonized with principalities in the mind, near death experiences close to ten times, dealing with the courts and going through a bitter divorce, having thoughts to kill with no remorse, I Am Reality; reality of forgiveness that's being forced, fasting and praying constantly astringing from sexual intercourse, that was a mental and spiritual healing, I became much stronger and gained more control of my feelings, studied, worshiped, lit candles before kneeling, I Am Reality; reality of being righteous as well as being a heathen, you see what I sowed as a child I later started reaping, I remember being deceiving perpetrating to the left my hat would be leaning, I tortured animals till they stopped breathing, headed the wrong way with no fears of being beaten, I got older and started seeing the things my dad was preaching, learning the hard way my wisdom way increasing, I gained love from tough love that had me deeply thinking, I Am Reality; reality of change and believing, the good and the bad, living life too fast, I hit rock bottom having everything to crash, I Am Reality; reality of those that arise from a disastrous past, having love and hate, a pistol pointed in my face, I had a strong urge to retaliate, leave em somewhere buried without a trace, I had my little son to think about, we couldn't bare for me to catch a case and leave him fatherless in this evil place, so I just wished that death would come and take him away, but was I wrong for feeling that way? After going through so many pains and heartaches, being placed in situations with no way to escape, I remember my car was faced the opposite way on the Bishop Ford expressway, coming head-on an 18-wheeler with no attempts to break, there was no time to pray, all I could do was bow my head and wait, but reality is; that Just Mic is still here today, living out my purpose and holding on to faith, I Am Reality; I am the reconciliation of all hate against enemies and race having your mind in a murdering-state, I Am Reality; I am that voice of the black nationality, all religions transformed to spirituality, I am the Book of Psalms with a Solomon's mentality, poetry deep inside of a poetic gallery, I am comfort to all of those that's lost someone to a fatality, from birth I was reality, dealt with situations throughout my years that rattled me, I maintained and became an inspiration to a Generation of realities, I am peace not war so don't try and battle me, you will lose anyway trying to mentally wrestle me, I've done spiritually died came back alive baptized with Calvary, I've lived lives on both sides, I Am Reality of all my realities, so who are you? Cause I Am Reality.

my testimony

"I Am Reality" is a poem that I was inspired to write from another poet and close friend of mine named (Jazzy Jazz). One evening he just approached me and told me to write something on reality; so I took it for granted at first because I always come up with my own titles. After a few days it stayed on my mind and I began to reflect back in my life. It was a moment when I just started being honest with myself about some of the most personal and devastating times that I've been through. This poem showed me a lot about who I was and helped me to realize how I persevered and overcame. "I Am Reality" let me know that through it all God was always with me.

JOB 9:20-21

If I justify myself, mine own mouth shall condemn me: if I say, I am perfect it shall also prove me perverse. Though I were perfect, yet would I not know my soul: I would despise my life.

"The game has its ups and downs, but you can never lose focus of your individual goals and you can't let yourself be beat because of lack of effort."
-Michael Jordan

Part Two: Love and Pain

<u>When You Let Me Go</u>

When You Let Me Go I moved on to a life that awaited me for years, I was blinded, trapped, but now everything seems more clear, it was like I was shackled in chains full of rage, going through a never ending phase that prevented me from the mics and the stage, little did I know that chapter was closed but I never flipped the page, I was drained, ashamed, in endless pain, left with a burden that only God could change, so I let go of pride and on myself I began to place the blame, I dropped to my knees and prayed and asked him to show me the way, you gave me the poem "My Father" that's still tattooed on my arm today, so I came back to a place that I always used to escape but this time it was for me to stay and show my people the way, I understand now When You Let Me Go it was meant because the world needed me more, he couldn't use me with my mind and soul in a mess, not loving myself and being depressed, so you gave me love and peace and a drive to speak poetic life with my breath, When You Let Me Go I couldn't sleep nor rest, but I had to be put through the test, so that in me you could bring out the best, I'm so free and full of life after being so close to death, When You Let Me Go I was down like the poverty of poor people, but only to become stronger and rise like the great white eagle, fly with my mission, dreams and visions, become that poetic soldier to make a difference, touch the lives of the ones that's dead but still living, write books to the minds that's mentally in prison, give a child hope that he or she can still finish, When You Let Me Go I lost but it was for me to start over again and now I realize that I'm winning, I'm more thankful of your decision now I'm more anointed and gifted, full of joy and grateful for the inner voice I listened, I'm living my purpose, letting him use me with service, I'll never look back, if I do it's to smile learn from my mistakes and of myself to be proud, When You Let Me Go I became a man and began to live again having fun like a child, I came from being distant to interacting with crowds, writing and producing tracks getting the love and support that I never had, I have no regrets, I live for today and look forward to what's next, you were meant to be an ex for me to prosper and be blessed and one day give it all to the next, it was hard but the past I left, it's funny now, it was like a play or a movie at the show, through it all it has made me who I am today and that's a poet with lyrical flow, ready and on the go moving forward to be some-ones next hero, to a mother or child that was told no, you see it was all designed for both, it was meant for me to change to help bring change When You Let Me Go.

my testimony

"When You Let Me Go" was inspired from my past marriage and divorce. It had me take time to look back and realize how I overcame and moved forward building a closer relationship with God. I then finally began to live a righteous and amazing life as an inspiring Writer, Host and Spoken Word Artist.

Proverbs 21:21

He that followeth after righteousness and mercy findeth life, righteousness, and honor.

She's Still Searching

She's Still Searching, for that one love She's Still Searching to heal her soul where she's been left hurting

She's getting tired of all these heartaches and pains, being left with just memories and names, some were liars, some were cheaters, while others were just controllers and beaters, never taking the blame, being over protective of your pretty frame, I may be a man but yet I can understand your pain, still searching you've been searching long, you see in-love is where your heart belongs, she's getting tired of playing these same sad songs, is there a right one? She's uncertain, not giving up just yet She's Still Searching

For that one love She's Still Searching to heal her soul where she's been left hurting, She's Still Searching, it's for that one love She's Still Searching

She's still wiping tears from her eyes, opening her heart to another angel in disguise, now it's different guys approaching you with the same lines, saying he's not like the others, she wasn't surprised, telling yourself to give him a try, you don't want true love to pass you by, keeping the faith you must, even though it seems hard to trust, it's no more player stuff taken, she's ready for real love making, her heart is guarded but yet it's still open, it's still scarred from all the times it's been left broken, left alone to raise her children she's stressed out from school and working, she always puts on a smile but its deep down inside that she's still hurting

37

POETIC SCRIPTURES (THE LIFE, GROWTH AND JOURNEY)

For that one love She's Still Searching to heal her soul where she's been left hurting, She's Still Searching, it's for that one love She's Still Searching

Her days are shorter, her nights are longer, you see no more of her ex's can call her, she don't really need a baller, learned how to be independent on her own, now she just needs a man that can hold his own, not afraid to open up and let his feelings be known, can hold her close after making her moan, can put the family first and stay by her side whenever times get worse, can be the man of the home and not take it to his head, he has confidence in himself but it's by God he's lead, admits when he's wrong and can stick to the vows that he said, until then she'll be hoping and praying, for that one love that will be permanently staying, after being physically abused and emotionally misused, with that one love she's still willing to choose, she's not yet closed the curtain, she's not giving up just yet, it's for that one love She's Still Searching.

my testimony

This is a poem that I was inspired to write after placing myself in a woman's shoes. Men including myself have taken relationships for granted and mistreated their mate by allowing our greed and self-control to over-take us. We have more than enough lost a good wife or girlfriend leaving her with heartaches and pains.

Psalms 57:2

I will cry unto God most high; unto God that performeth all things for me.

Come Take Me Away

Somebody please Come Take Me Away, don't get me wrong at times it's cool being single but I'm not trying to stay in that same mental-state, I need you here I'm getting tired of making my own dinner plates, though I know we have to be on the same page and pace, it's been a while but with patience I wait, I read and take caution I'm not trying to catch no case, she has to be mental, physical and spiritually straight, somebody please

Come Take Me Away

We on the same page politically we relate, but not too deep, on our own lives we concentrate, on different ways we can bring change, she has to be strong in faith, enjoys the finer things but not too material-based, she understands how to live her dreams and not chase, I'm holding on but somebody please

Come Take Me Away

Spend a little time let's elope out the states, study, fast and together we pray, toast to the end of a lonely life and forever we stay, when they see us they see double but we become one as we join as a couple, we huddle, we fight in the trenches in the times of struggle, somebody please

Come Take Me Away

Show me something different, make my home my favorite place, save me from the pillow in the case, the times that I waste on "Just Mic's Hell Date's," this is a public service announcement, she has to be well-grounded, classy but not too flashy, she doesn't have to know everything, you can feel free to just ask me, proud but not too much pride, we don't have to drive all the time, we can ride our bikes together, catch the train up north and bless mics together, become Beyoncé and Jay but hardly apart, never taking it for granted there's no time to waste, I got my heart slipping out one hand and my soul in the other, somebody please

Come Take Me Away

I'm not that brotha that needs his summers, we can walk the beach, you can even smother me, I don't mind I need to catch up on all the lonely times, when true love was hard to find, so whatever's on your mind I'm here to listen, I don't care about the other ladies outside with hips and thighs, you have my undivided attention, so let's trade applications and skip the dating, fall deep in-love, I'm here I crave for you each day, somebody please

Come Take Me Away

my testimony

"Come Take Me Away" was inspired from just being single for the past five years or so. That time was spent focusing on self-growth, but at times I did feel alone. I couldn't help to think of how it would be to have that rib by my side.

Genesis 2:18

And the Lord said, "It is not good that man should be alone; I will make him an help meet for him."

Worth the Wait

Worth the Wait, I often wonder is true love Worth the Wait, they say good things come to those that wait, awake forever taking the place of my worthless dates, I wonder, I know she will be great, greater than my last mate that prepared me to travel never ending love that I face, I know it's much needed with so much hate, in the world, I know within her I can deeply escape, enjoy the never ending pleasures as we both embrace, live in our own little heaven on earth, they say this life is what you make it, it's been a while since I've cared so deep or had feelings and thinking about how nice of a couple we would be, making each other laugh and writing poetry, helping one-another and being unique, I no longer wonder I just think how my new life will be; a kiss, a hug, the day we meet and greet on our first date, a surprise or treat, the day we hold hands and promise one to keep, walk the isle and take that leap, make passionate love and one day start a family, I know it's going to take strength, patience and prayer but I believe from each other we can learn and teach, I know we can endure with faith, so yes I'll wait, for her I know it will be Worth the Wait.

my testimony

I was inspired to write this poem because at times I want to settle to prevent from being alone, but I know that God wants me to have all that he has for me if I just be patient and wait.

Proverbs 19:22

Whoso findeth a wife findeth a good thing, and obtaineth favour of the lord.

True Love

True Love, I question do many of us even know what it is?
Some of us still suffer from hurts and wonder if it even exist
Well I don't believe it ever did at least in my relationships
But I do believe that it's somewhere out there
Waiting for me to heal from all the broken wounds that only
True Love can fix
So I stay wondering and fantasize with deep imaginations of
a passionate kiss
One that I can say I just know this is it
With True Love there's no such thing as taking a risk
This would be a life-long reality that others just wish
It's too often that we fall into situations that would have us
to give up and just quit
And on the right one we miss
Overlooking the True Love, the True Love that may come
only once in a lifetime
The True Love they say is hard to find
And it is because how can we love another and still have
hate of what the last mate did?
It's with burdens, pains and heartaches that we tend to live
Un-forgiveness that leads to another bitter relationship
Never letting go of what the last soul left inside
We move on to the next and keep those feelings hid; never
healing with time
True Love I believe would wait and let go
Not having the next to suffer from the past that never died
We want to be loved and nurtured
Cared for, for them to give us their all and let down their
walls
Begin to fall deep in-love with a heart that still needs to
mend
True Love waits, its long-suffering, its patient and kind

It's also felt from both at the same time
True Love releases stress from the mind
It's faithful and never lies
True Love cries, no matter the gender
It remains sweet and becomes stern when it needs to be
It does not hold beefs or feels that it needs to verbal abuse and mistreat
True Love brings peace and a life more abundantly
A love that you will always feel the need to keep
It never disappears or feels the need for a break
It just anticipates the love from the time that's spent away
It doesn't let one day just pass and not hear or see the others face
True Love makes time to put a smile on that special some-ones face
When they smile, you smile feeling joyful doing things just in-case
Never taking the other for granted
We live for the time that we make
True Love will always be at the right time and right place.

my testimony

"True Love" was inspired from a particular Valentine's Day in 2014. I would reminisce back on prior relationships realizing why they never worked out, and it was simple, because True Love didn't exist. At-least within my relationships it didn't. I believe that True Love is the love of God that comes through a person and will be everlasting.

Ephesians 5: 22-25

Wives, submit yourselves unto your husbands, as unto the Lord. For the husband is the head of the wife, as also Christ is the head of the church; and He is the Savior of the body. Therefore, just church is subject unto Christ, so let the wives be to their own husbands in everything. Husbands love your wives, just as Christ also loved the church and gave Himself for her.

My Father

My Father I know that without you I just can't make it, "God is my refuge and strength" in your word those words are stated and how true that is, wanting to give up but it's you that still wants me to live, it's all of my heart, mind and soul that you want me to give, and it hurts to be forced into a corner with no one to talk to but you, no one to understand or listen but you, My Father I realize that what's been missing is you, I need you to walk with me and guide my steps, just steer me straight cause without you I seem to go right and left, then you have to whip me back in line, and it hurts cause I still feel the wepts, but through it all it's my mind that you kept, losing my bride that you have given to me, it's every day that I'm becoming more and more weak, needing you so that I'm able to stand on my own two feet, "My Father which art in heaven I'm calling out your name" just take away my every hurt and pain, fill me with joy and laughter, or whatever you feel that I need, it doesn't even matter, only you know what's best for me, Father I'm just not myself, I need you to be the rest of me, give me all of your spirit to bring out the best in me, at times I just get tired of praying, my thoughts keep drifting, I know it's time Father, so just give me that refilling, that strength to keep my hands lifted, more patience and faith to know that the times will be shifted, the man that I'm becoming he will be different, more understanding cause I've prayed for it, more wisdom and knowledge cause I've craved for it, it's been too often that I've heard your voice and ignored it, please forgive me Father cause everything I've lost I need you to restore it, I need your grace and mercy even though it feels as if I'm not even worthy, and I hate to think that cause on the inside it really hurts me, a young man about to be two years past thirty, I know you have a calling on my life rather that's with or without a wife, only you know my desires and what's on the inside that's hid and it has to come out while I live, I need you to replace or give me back my rib, but in the meantime be a wife to me, comfort me through the night, put your arms around me and show me what's right, teach me how to love like Christ, My Father I need you to stay with me all the days of my life, prepare me cause I don't know what's ahead and I do trust you, I'm brave but somehow I'm still afraid, awakened in the morning not wanting to face the days and that's sometimes even after I've prayed, but every day you seem to see me through it, letting me know that you still care, that I'm still your child and whenever I call you'll still be there, My Father thank you for everything you have blessed me with, my health, my strength, being able to see with my eyes and all of my gifts, I love you Father even though I don't show it enough but just stay with me, cause lately it's been rough, you're the only one that understands you know exactly what I'm dealing with as a man, it's your will, I just have to follow the plan, to take away every evil and unrighteous thoughts that come to my mind, fill my spirit with joy, peace and positivity, just let your word sink into me, let it shine, let it glow, within my words just have it to flow, within my walk and talk have it to show,

POETIC SCRIPTURES (THE LIFE, GROWTH AND JOURNEY)

My Father I'm just letting my feelings be known, it seems like all my life I've been wrong, so just stay with me cause I just can't make it alone.

my testimony

"My Father" was written during the time that I was going through a divorce after being married for five years. I was forced into a corner with a desperate need of comfort and guidance. God had me to write and I began to re-evaluate my life and to put him first. So through it all by me humbling my-self and going to him in prayer it helped me to pray more. Through this I was able to build a relationship with my spiritual Father.

Romans 8:38

For I am persuaded that neither death, nor life, nor angels, nor principalities, nor powers, nor things to come, nor height, nor depth, nor any other creature, shall be able to separate us from the love of God which is in Christ Jesus our Lord.

Only Begotten Son

You are that light, spark and motivation, for me to live life
to its fullest
Accomplish all my dreams and goals
Work hard preparing my events and shows
You were born for many reasons beyond the ones that I
know
So cleaver and smart it's like you've been here before
I often think of having a second child
And I wonder would I love you more
My Only Begotten Son, my first born
It's so amazing to watch you grow and age
Wanting to be like me having passions to entertain
But I want you to be you and be better with all that you do
And always be brave
Many ask why I never gave you my first name
I never wanted us to get mixed up with identities just in-
case I never changed
But I did and I thank God for you, a love that he gave me
My life will never be the same
I recall not loving myself for decisions that I had made
I felt like giving up but you were the only reason that I stayed
That night I prayed, I was shown that you were meant to
guide my ways
An angel, a prophet, a child with adult knowledge
Showing me things that I may not even know or understand
Through the years we've learned from one-another
I know I'm your dad, but at times you feel like a friend or
little brother
But don't get it twisted
Remember to always obey and respect me as well as your
mother
Be a great leader and never follow others

POETIC SCRIPTURES (THE LIFE, GROWTH AND JOURNEY)

Research, study and learn
Go for what you desire and make sure it's well earned
Wisely spend your time not just on video games and DVDs
pushing rewind
Don't always be told what to do, be more responsible
Wash dishes and clean your room
I know you are always hungry, but don't eat so much
Try just breakfast, dinner and a small lunch
And I noticed your love for basketball
It may seem easy now, but these other children are growing
fast
And because of me you might not be that tall
If so, work with what you have, your strength, your speed
and moves with the ball
It starts now that you must strive to be the best
Do all your homework and study for every test
Keep playing the mind games, scramble and chess
Don't wear yourself out so much always take time to rest
Pray, save your money and never make bets
Unless, it's with me and we going for a dream that we both
trying to catch
I know at times I'm not around
But I anticipate our times and look forward to having fun
Know that I love you much
My Only Begotten Son!

my testimony

"Only Begotten Son" was inspired from the times that I'm away from my son (Elijah). I wanted him to know and understand that he has purpose in life and that he can be all that he can be. He must start at an early age and not waste time as I did when I was younger.

Proverbs 15:20
A wise son maketh a glad father: but a foolish man despiseth his mother.

"If you learn late, you pass it on to people so they can learn early. It's a step process."

-Russell Simmons

<u>Part Three: Growth and Inspiration</u>

Imagine, Vision and Dream

I've done sacrificed and prayed I've shed all my tears, now humble and brave it's like I decayed all my fears, letting go of the past I'm looking forward to the upcoming years, but as I rewind into time it was a little rough in 2009, feeling like I've lost all my life, my wife, through death my sister, some more kin and close friends, burdened no longer I've gotten much stronger since then, staying dedicated and faithful to God I can't do nothing but win, with my shield and my sword we gone battle this thing to the end, it's a new Mike a new life with Christ in the year 2010, wait a minute, "shut up devil I'm gone release every thought as I write with this pen, all the pain and all the pressure, it's been a long time but I'm finally getting it together," as I sit through the sermons I listen, everything that's wrong I have to fix it, staying on that grind man I'm so hungry and vicious, moving every mountain I got to clear my vision, I'm breaking through chains as if I was locked-up in prison, I'm coming out of a storm, getting closer to my destiny I'm becoming lukewarm, every thought, every vision and dream, I got enough faith to believe, enough strength if nobody ever joins my team, pats me on the back and tell me to go ahead and do my thing, I got enough courage no matter how difficult it may seem; now excuse me as I scream, but don't get it twisted I'm not crazy or mean, like (Kevin Garnett) I had to let off a little tension and steam, cause I can't look back, leave the past in the past and work on the present cause every struggle is a lesson, gotta still beware cause everyday I'm gone be tested, so it's on my knees and my word is where my times invested, I know with God rolling the dice it's only seven and eleven, I'm gone win this race, people take heed take the Most High lead if you plan on catching, I'm in a zone, I fall asleep with rhymes and wake up poetic it's no time for resting, I can't wait, I can't sit around doing nothing, like (Outkast) I gotta get up, get out and get something, again life done knocked me down but I'm back up punching, and it's rough being alone but I'm slowly adjusting, I'm good because it's not my will it's in his that I'm trusting, no room for negativity you can get away from me don't tell me nothing, I'm staying focused and I don't wanna hear it, you see my attitude has changed and my priorities are different, I'm thinking positivity cause I'm lead by the spirit, I'm taking no credit that I'm anointed with lyrics, cause inside my temple is where my church is, inside these four walls is where my service is, I'm finally realizing what my purpose is, to be that inspiration to these youngsters and kids, that hope if you've given up and no longer wanna live, still broken hearted after giving all that you can give, I just wanna give that same encouragement that I needed, that same faith when I didn't believe, being down and out I needed spiritual treatment, I hurt like you hurt, at the end of the tunnel I couldn't see it, but I was only going through phases of life, so stay in the fight it's gone be alright, just be wise with every decision," think twice is this actually worth risking"? I thought I would lose my freedom and wind up in prison, I can't keep going through life knowing that God is still missing, can't keep coming to church and not striving to live as a Christian, fellas is it worth your marriage and your family by going out tricking, gangs and drugs homie you need to think about quitting, cause it's an education and learning that makes you grown, those choices will lead you quick to a funeral home, my sisters be strong it's been years that you been doing it on your own, being that mother and that father at home, if you don't have a shoulder, here; just take a few of my words to lean on or when you get home take out them slow-jams and put on that favorite gospel song, you may be lonely but know that you are not alone, in closing; I want to wish the best for all of yall, take nothing for granted cause you never know when he may call, during this life you slip you fall but get back up and stand tall, you gone walk again but until then it's ok to crawl, so just stick to them plans and believe, set goals to achieve, just Imagine, Vision and Dream, stay away from the poisonous things, go after what you want and pray for what you need, just put God first with everything; never give up and you will succeed!

my testimony

I was inspired to write "Imagine, Vision and Dream" after being away from poetry and writing for over 10 years. I was going through some very challenging times in life and I really needed something to inspire myself and to take my life in another direction. I used this poem and the experiences that I've been through to encourage myself and uplift others.

ECCLESIASTES 3:1

To everything there is a season, and a time to every purpose under the heaven.

I'm Gone Keep Going

Being a man of God how can I be silent, but it's gone take more than me to speak to try and stop this violence, we keep marching but it's still not enough, come one yall let's start thinking, I know it's tough but these streets are getting way too rough, its too many of us with our minds stuck and corrupt, shooting guns believing that's the way to be tough, and if I don't I'm a punk, come on yall you got it all mixed up, it's no guns in jail you gone be forced to throw a punch, just take this life slow don't be in such a rush, I just want to stop you before they put you in handcuffs, I'm reaching out I know it's at least one I could touch

But I'm Gone Keep Going and I'm gone keep fighting, pulling, scratching and biting like Mike Tyson, I can't stop now I got minds to enlighten, scrapbooks still in drawers from when I first started writing, words never put together and never re-sighted, I can't stop now it's too many youngsters living with no guidance

They say it's the X-Generation, but come on yall help me to change it to be more like a Christian Nation, let's start forming our own organizations, it's getting serious more of a spiritual war that we facing, dealing with minds that's done turned straight reprobating, you got to be in line with God now cause you don't know who in the world you dating, my young people it's time to awaken, stop all this jealousy and hatin on our own women degrading, don't wanna work hard for nothing we just wanna take it, I'm praying even more now for my little son to make it, it's so evil it seem like everybody faking, but with my voice and my words that was once taken, I'm gone put it to use and spread it all across the nation, if yall not with me I'll grab these little kids to help me change it, write em all songs to sing and have you all worship and praising

But I'm Gone Keep Going and I'm gone keep fighting, pulling, scratching and biting like Mike Tyson, I can't stop now I got minds to enlighten, scrapbooks still in drawers from when I first started writing, words never put together, and never re-sighted, I can't stop now it's too many youngsters living with no guidance

You see Just Mic wanna help every lost individual, before we're holding candles at another prayer visual, we getting used to it, it seems like nobody cares, looking down under the tree surrounded by flowers and teddy-bears, rather than trying to figure was it meant, we need to figure better ways that it can be prevent, stop being afraid and step up and try to change this because it's all ridiculous, every weekend we filling up Gatling's List, another youngster gone it don't make no sense, and I don't mean to get all deep tense but I was given a gift to uplift from the Most High that I've been rolling with, and I wanna take you with me and build a better relationship, believe me it's no myth it took me 33 years to finally realize this

And I'm Gone Keep Going, I'm gone keep fighting, pulling, scratching and biting like Mike Tyson, I can't stop now I got minds to enlighten, scrapbooks still in drawers from when I first started writing, words never put together and never re-

sighted, I can't stop now it's too many youngsters living with no guidance.

my testimony

"I'm Gone Keep Going" was inspired one night after getting off work and catching the bus home from 95th and the Dan Ryan. I remember looking down at the expressway and watching the cars and trucks ride past. The traffic never stopped it just kept going and going. I realized that I needed to keep going with my writing and to help bring change in any way that I can. With the rise of violence in Chicago I wanted to take things to another level. I also didn't want to just write about what was going on but to be more of an activist and help bring peace.

Matthew 5:9

Blessed are the peacemakers: for they shall be called the children of God.

POETIC SCRIPTURES (THE LIFE, GROWTH AND JOURNEY)

I Am Not Afraid

I Am Not Afraid
I now work for rewards that's beyond this life and the grave
With every line and time that I grab the mic and brace the stage
I leave behind words to those that's psychologically slaved
Daily I grind and search for ways to bring change
I squash beefs, build and poetically teach
Use all of my gifts to be the best inspiration that I can be
Write till my last breath and leave behind a legacy

I Am Not Afraid

We as poets, lyricist, and authors have to speak
This is what our ancestors died for; or freedom and speech
So let's become one army fight and win back our neighborhoods and streets
Why are we becoming so weak?
Being divided because of beliefs
We must use what we have to help the next see through it
With this one life to live we should wisely choose it
Study, pray and find ways to improve it
With each day we age we stay stuck in our ways so afraid of change

I Am Not Afraid

My ladies we must be brave
I know you've been hurt and abused with lies
Feeling as if you can't survive; without a man by your side
You must learn to move on and leave the past behind
Find that strength on the inside that our late Queens had

POETIC SCRIPTURES (THE LIFE, GROWTH AND JOURNEY)

Together you all must rise and keep the Lord by your side
He is your light and salvation don't be afraid

I Am Not Afraid

My Brothers we don't have to be so tough and hard
Following the next man that's headed behind bars
Be a leader and create on your own
Make the schools and library your second home
You don't have to do crimes and smoke weed all the time
Take control of your future and empower your minds
Before losing it and can never rewind
You still young and you still have time
You can survive without drugs, AK's and Nines
Stop saying that's all you know
You got brothas like Obama and I giving you hope
X and King that came b4
They didn't lose they lives so that you can destroy and take mine
Making it less and less men to build families and make our ladies brides
In reality inside I'm crying, cause daily we dying and losing young lives
But I'm here for change and I'm brave
I will not quit cause

I Am Not Afraid

my testimony

"I Am Not Afraid" was inspired during Black History Month of 2014. I was just looking back on how far we have come as a people (African Americans). I realize how they stood up for us back then and how they were not afraid to speak out or help bring unity and change.

Psalms 27:1
The Lord is my light and my salvation; whom shall I fear?
The Lord is the strength of my life; of whom shall I be afraid?

POETIC SCRIPTURES (THE LIFE, GROWTH AND JOURNEY)

The Day I Found You

I remember being broken and torn having no joy and direction
I was a young man full of oppression
Lost with no guidance going from church to church
And at times I just stayed home because I didn't want to show my tears from being so hurt
Afraid to look in the mirror cause all I saw was the worst
I tried to read and pray on my own but it still wouldn't work
The Day I Found You; it was like I was being nursed
Slowly putting back all the pieces to finally end my soul search
I can still remember that Sunday when I came in empty and left with no thirst
You showed me that I was still his child but I never put him first
After growing up and being raised in the church
I was saved but not saved by grace
I always did it my way; The Day I Found You it restored my faith
Took me to a higher spiritual-state
Instead of judging others, I judged myself and took in all the word that I could take
Instead of anger and hate love and joy was replaced
I learned patience and on God how to wait
I stop dwelling on my past it had become a life that I erased
The Day I Found You; you showed me to take it day by day
Every smile, song, hug, and confirmation in word made me stay
All of my goals and dreams, you showed me that it wasn't too late
Without you I don't know where I would be
Probably sitting in another church far in the back seat

POETIC SCRIPTURES (THE LIFE, GROWTH AND JOURNEY)

Falling asleep or seeing who my next girlfriend could be
Never operating in my calling and doing ministry, never learning dedication and loyalty
But steadily repeating a cycle that would end up costing me
The Day I Found You
I gradually became free, free from the mind that a woman can't Pastor, Teach, or Preach
I know for myself because I became strong after being so weak
Without each sermon I wouldn't be Just Mic spitting heat
So brave and not afraid of the enemy, I can do all things through Christ who strengthens me
I've heard it said again and again but SBG showed me that that means nothing if you have no belief
All my life I was left in defeat
But now I soar to excel and over mountains I leap; The Day I Found You
I found my inner peace; I will inherit the earth by being humble and meek
I no longer live in darkness because you allowed me to see
On higher grounds I now place my feet, for no one else can I speak
I just know for myself what SBG has done for me
Really allowed me to prosper and grow, help bring others together
And bring out gifts that they were afraid to show
Showed me love and helped me in times of need
Prioritized the important things and how to plant my spiritual seeds
The Day I Found You
I found healing from when my heart would bleed
I've learned leadership and how by example that I can also lead

POETIC SCRIPTURES (THE LIFE, GROWTH AND JOURNEY)

And each day I strive, I understand now that wisdom and knowledge comes with time
So I never stop learning or get comfortable of where I'm at
Yea SBG taught me that
I love them dearly and need them to survive
I say that a lot because I know that it's true
Every week I'm touched and inspired no matter what I may be going through
I know I'm with a ministry that loves and cares
They are the ones that I remember when no one else was there
They showed me it's going to still be some bumps in the road
And that it's not always fair, if I'm losing it's not yet over
If I need a place of comfort I can rest on their shoulders
And if there is an army rising up it's the SBG soldiers
They not all the same but their real and true
They think of themselves no higher and try to bring the best out of you
Saved by Grace I will always remember; The Day I Found You!

my testimony

"The Day I Found You" was a poem that was dedicated to my church home Saved by Grace Kingdom Ministries International. After being disconnected from having a strong relationship with God, he showed me that I needed to continue to grow spiritually and that I needed leadership. Since joining SBG my life hasn't been the same. It was all by his divine plan to elevate my life and to be an inspiration to others.

Proverbs 11:30

The fruit of the righteous is the tree of life; and he that winneth souls is wise.

POETIC SCRIPTURES (THE LIFE, GROWTH AND JOURNEY)

Always Have a Dream

You must see more than a dark cloud
The same block, a siren after gun sounds
But a young man shining with a smile
Not ashamed on the inside but proud
Proud to be who; he is
Looking to the future
And not back on the wrong that he did
Having a heart of integrity
Dreaming on, pushing on after what's been said to me
This is for that he, that she
Rather you bound or free
Still fighting the streets
Always Have a Dream
No matter the picture that's seen
Perhaps similar to Martin Luther King
You can be that Teacher, that Singer
Write books, become a Motivational Speaker
Be your own believer
Like Nike just do it
Put God first and put your mind to it
Don't give up
Cause you gone get through it
I know I can, Satan can't stop me
And neither can this human called man
The government system
As long as I have a mind of my own
Seek knowledge and wisdom
Always Have a Dream to be more than a crack fiend
Doing sins to make your green
The righteous way is right
Even though it's stress and hell in this life
Always Have a Dream of an after life

POETIC SCRIPTURES (THE LIFE, GROWTH AND JOURNEY)

Fear and doubt is darkness
But to be brave with faith is light
Stay humble and on that spiritual side
Be prayerful and let your self-conscience guide
Always dream of a family
A groom or bride
Better neighborhoods a more peaceful side
I dream the soldiers safely arrive
And never go back in the predicament of suicide
I dream we all know the truth from the lies
I dream for parentless children to arise
Be they own parents
To one day erase their hurts and cries
I dream of a more passionate generation
Less stereotyping and salary basing
More love and less hating
I dream of a traditional change
Where every race can hang
All churches combine to sing
Always Have a Dream
U can stop being that dealer
You haven't been caught yet
You can stop being that killer
Your grandmother done prayed
Just know that most heroes are in the grave
So stay alive so you can tell your story
You've been blessed
Always dream to resurrect your mind and flesh
You have those skills you might as well be the best
Of your abilities you must think no-less
Forget the critics, look at them as midgets
Because they will never reach your destiny
They will never reach your treasury
Rather if it's in your pocket or in spirit

POETIC SCRIPTURES (THE LIFE, GROWTH AND JOURNEY)

The negative thoughts you have to clear it
Flip them cards you've been dealt
If no one believes in you, believe in yourself
Don't give up; trying hard is not trying hard enough
Be your own leader
Be your own inspiration
No matter the picture that's seen
Remember to Always Have a Dream

my testimony

This poem was inspired after someone told me that I would never write a book. Instead of feeding into that negativity it actually motivated me more to write and work towards becoming a Published Author.

2 Philippians 4:13
I can do all things through Christ who strengthens me.

Be Like Jesus

This man that I am he keeps making mistakes, falling off the tracks not staying focused and straight, you keep whipping me back in line you keep giving me breaks, just not being patient and willing to wait, forgetting to pray and coming to church too late, there's no hiding there's no way to escape, you keep touching me, I feel your spirit and vision your face, it's in that high place that you want me to stay, away from being carnal and wrapped up in that spiritual-state, now what will it take? you've given me mercy and you've given me grace, much love and had all my sins erased, when I was angered you took away all the hate, knowing that I could of easily caught a case, with my life and my freedom at stake you stepped in and had me to pray, put the right people in my life and given me wisdom and faith, I owe my life to you, I owe my time to you, every rhyme and every dime to you, and it's not just me Lord, we need you to reach us, we need you to teach us, to stay by our side and in your word to feed us

Time is winding up and I just wanna Be Like Jesus, I just wanna Be Like Jesus, I just wanna Be Like Jesus, every day, every month of the year, I just wanna Be Like Jesus

Now humble me Lord, give me strength and power, camp your angel's around me every minute and every hour, just have me to keep that sound mind, peace and joy and to follow life in your design, use me I don't won't nobody to be left behind, they trying but give them a little more time, the world is lost with the blind leading the blind, but upon us just have your light to shine to step in between that it may open their eyes, "Just walk with me, hold my hand and stay by my side, I need you to be more long-suffering and to be a bit more kind and to speak the truth" yea you right because when I don't it's just like I'm lying, knowing that we just got one life, one choice, one time, so don't be afraid to step out in that isle and get in that line, he's using me he's trying to reach us and he will soon be coming for the true believers

Time is winding up and I just wanna Be Like Jesus, I just wanna Be Like Jesus, I just wanna Be Like Jesus, every day, every month of the year, I just wanna Be Like Jesus!

POETIC SCRIPTURES (THE LIFE, GROWTH AND JOURNEY)

my testimony

I was inspired to write this poem after one of the sermons that my Pastor had preached. The message was about being more Christ-Like and not being afraid to let your light shine.

COLOSSIANS 3:12

Put on therefore, as the elect of God, holy and beloved, bowels of mercies, kindness, humbleness of mind, meekness, longsuffering;

POETIC SCRIPTURES (THE LIFE, GROWTH AND JOURNEY)

I Am a Poet

I Am a Poet, with emotions of anger, pain, and tears
Poetic poems were being built inside of me for 21 years
It just took the sacrifice of my baby-sister for me to begin to relive
Looking back reflecting on my life I began to write
Letters, songs, poems, my own Poetic Scriptures
As each poem would change so did the man in the mirror
Filling up the pages I began to release my temper
Mad at myself for staying hid behind the chair and the clippers
Knowing that "I Am a Poet," what you saw then was a man that was growing
And going through the difficulties of life,
I was being groomed and molded
Into a better man and a better poet, creating poetry of healing and spiritual power
I would spend long night's hour after hour
Just me, my pen and my pad
I was obsessed
Up under my eyes became bags
I wrote more than John and Paul with their lines forwarded and tagged
A Freedom Writer, a person of extraordinary talent
An Author in the making
I would fill up the notebook pages
But it was all for nothing, until I hit the stages
All that was hid and written was finally spoken
Words of truth, reality and life
You see I'll never forget the night when I met (Articulite)
I was featured at "Livin Clean" and since that night
I began to step on the scene and bless the mics
I ran across (Jeronimo), he told me to link up with (Blaq Ice)

POETIC SCRIPTURES (THE LIFE, GROWTH AND JOURNEY)

So for months I studied the set
But the first night I knew it was right
I saw family, love and unity
All black shirts with P.O.E.T in purity white
I was a force on my own but I needed more might
Something to hold me up because I was getting too light
Feeling alone on the battlefield
It was the old me and Just Mic
I needed a King to take me under the wings
To fulfill dreams and purpose in life
It's no more turning back
Cause every vision and dream is coming to life
So from this day forward, for P.O.E.T; I will fight
For our lost children; I will fight
From this day forward for my son I will live my life
I will speak love and peace and bring more souls to Christ
If it takes me seven years I will wait for a holy and virtuous
wife
You can call me crazy, but "I Am a Poet"
That deserves the best because I've sacrificed
And I'm striving righteously to live my life
I'm now on a poetic mission
And for every public library; I will write
For church sanctuaries; I will write
For gangsters on obituaries, I will write
I will help bring the dream of Martin Luther King to life
I was born to be one of poetries favorites
To prevent our youth from dying young and being locked in
the cages
My voice will be heard throughout this City and the Nations
"I Am a Poet" that will be remembered for ages
Known for taking a stand and making changes
I will write a song to heal the Generations
I will speak poetic Psalms to decrease the hatred

POETIC SCRIPTURES (THE LIFE, GROWTH AND JOURNEY)

*My next album "Save R Children, Save Our Streets" will be
highly anticipated*
I will become a poet's poet and a fans favorite
*Can't nothing stop me because in my mind I've already
made; it*
These poetic poems you better download and save it
"I Am a Poet" that has patiently waited
*But I'm here now, and I give honor to the poets that have
paved it*
I give thanks to God for my life
Cause through poetry he saved it
You see I'm not trying to be the coldest
I'm just speaking what he has given to me
The same way he did through Moses
From the day I was born I was chosen
And what is destined shall be
What has been prophesied to me daily; it's Unfolding
It's not a game that's why I don't smile in my poses
But I will on tonight cause in-case you haven't noticed

I Am a Poet!

my testimony

"I Am a Poet" was inspired first from my P.O.E.T organization (People of Extraordinary Talent). We were all asked to write a poem about us being a poet. I basically just looked at how I first came about writing and what got me inspired to perform and be passionate about my work.

Ecclesiastes: 3:1
To everything there is a season, and a time to every purpose under the heaven:

POETIC SCRIPTURES (THE LIFE, GROWTH AND JOURNEY)

Biography

Michael E. Williams also known as Just Mic "Da Poet," is an Inspirational Spoken Word Life Artist and Lyricist. He is known for having many different styles and voices while performing on stage. Just Mic shares many gifts and passions; as a Mentor, Host, Coach, Songwriter and Performer. Within just two years now Just Mic has created several platforms and opportunities for other up and coming artists to be heard. He takes a lot of pride in his work and is always looking to grow and working on new ideas to help bring change to different communities throughout Chicago as well as the world.

The Beginning

Michael E. Williams was born January of 1978, on the South Side of Chicago (Roseland). Due to the high rise of crime and violence his parents moved to South Suburban Dolton in the early 80's. With hopes of a better upbringing, Michael still was arrested and jailed several times as a juvenile. He eventually began to wake up and take his education and life more seriously. With no instruction he developed the gift of Barbering at the age of 16. After graduating from Thornridge High School he immediately went on to Cain's Barber College in 1997. It was just two years later that he would discover his love and passionate gift. Unfortunately, it came from the sudden death of his younger sister Larenya, who passed on March 19th of 1999. Two months after her passing Michael wrote her a letter titled, "A Letter to Baby-Sister". Since that day he has gone on to write hundreds of songs and poems.

The Birth of Just Mic

After battling through life's adversities and hardships Just Mic began to act out and perform his written and hidden poetry. Off and on through the years he performed on stages, but in the summer of (2012), Just Mic decided to enter into a Spoken Word competition. Even though he didn't place he was offered to be a featured artist at (Living Clean Poetry), a gospel poetry set on the South West side of Chicago. To get more prepared Just Mic wrote and produced his first Spoken Word Album (My Poetry) as well as his first spoken word video "Imagine, Vision and Dream" while taking a trip to Atlanta, Georgia. After returning to Chicago and being featured he was inspired to perform more often spending his time investing and working on being more of a Spoken Word Artist. Since that night he has not looked back. He has gone on to be featured at numerous of poetry concerts, shows, and events. Just Mic has also performed and interviewed live on several radio stations 102.3FM, 1570AM, 1390AM, 88.9FM Fusion Radio, Youth Speak Out and TCM. Just Mic has also performed live on TV Channel 19 as well as Channel 26 THEUTOO (Hot Sauce Poetry Series). In the year of (2013) he joined forces with P.O.E.T and was awarded as the (Best New Poet) as well as the (Host Award) for directing and hosting his own open mic events at the Harvey Public Library, Carter G. Woodson as well as at his Church in Hammond Indiana. In February of 2014, Just Mic was honored the featured artist and Poetic Inspiration in 3:16 Gospel Magazine. In April (2014) he also released his first single the heart felt testimony "I Am Reality" making it available for purchase worldwide on CD Baby Music Store. In November of (2014), Michael was awarded as one of the (Princes of Poetry) at the Heirs to The Throne Concert. He also became a first time

Published Author in December (2014) in The P.O.E.T Anthology Vol. 3 (Changing the World One Heart, One Mind, and One Voice at a Time). Just Mic has now created his own Non-for-Profit organization called P.O.M (Poetic Outreach Movement), set up to give youth an outlet to learn team building, self-esteem and conflict resolution skills through arts. Just Mic loves what he does and takes his desires to outreach very seriously. He hopes to one day open his own community center. Michael says "never set limits on yourself, to focus on now and continue to grow."

"Throughout my journey, life has been like a chain reaction, a lot of decisions and choices that I've made has caused me and others to either go forward or backwards. We are all put on this earth for a purpose and to fulfill a task in life. You are talented and gifted at something, once you discover and find out what it is; you must work to the fullest, giving it your all. It is very important what you do with your abilities, because they are not just for you to prosper and to grow, but to help inspire the next person to reach their destiny as well."

-Michael E. Williams a.k.a. Just Mic Da Poet

"I can never be where I ought to be until you are where you ought to be. We are interdependent."

-Dr. Martin Luther King Jr.

Contact Information:

For Booking: (773) 310-8219

Email: mike.williams42@ymail.com

Facebook: Mike Williams (Jus Mic)

Facebook Fan Page: Just Mic "Da Poet"

Purchase/Listen to Music:
Just Mic "Da Poet" @ CD Baby Music Store

Also available on Soundcloud and Reverbnation

Made in the USA
Charleston, SC
09 March 2016